365
Self-Improvement
Tips

Book 1

Sue Feldman

MORNING ROUTINE
Ideas

This book belongs to:

____

____

____

Gratitude

Gratitude is practice: If you want to lose weight, you exercise; if you want a happier life, be more grateful for what you have.

When you focus on what you have and appreciate it, you will live a happier life.

Practice gratitude every day, and you will have more to be grateful for.

Appreciate the smallest of things in life as it can lead to some of the biggest rewards.

Start each day with a gratitude list. Name three things for which you are grateful. It helps to put things into perspective.

Self-gratitude is often the hardest. Each day, write down something about yourself for which you are grateful.

When you feel anxious or angry, take a closer look at nature. Nature has a way of soothing the soul.

Express your gratitude daily to people in your life and watch your relationships flourish.

Instead of focusing on what you do not have, take plenty of time to focus on what you do have.

To be grateful you need to understand what you have. Acknowledge the challenging times to develop a sense of appreciation. Without the bad or tough times, you would have nothing to compare the good times to.

Use visual reminders, such as photos, to trigger appreciation for what you have been able to experience in your life.

Do not focus on yourself but on others. Gratitude is being thankful for what others have done for you or on your behalf.

When someone does something kind or thoughtful for you, show your gratitude by returning the gift with a heart-felt, "thank you."

Do not exaggerate your gratitude. When you express gratitude, keep it simple, honest, and to the point. Then move on. When you go on and on, it can be embarrassing, which is counterproductive.

Thanking the people who helped you to accomplish something is wonderful. However, do not downplay your role in your own success. If you have trouble accepting part of the credit, you may have low self-esteem.

Being able to see the positives is good. But do not gloss over an unpleasant situation because you think you should be grateful for everything. Denying that there is a problem will not fix anything or make you feel better.

Generosity and gratitude are different sides of the same coin. One side is what the giver feels, and the other is what the receiver feels. Regardless of which you start with you will end up feeling both, which leads to a feeling of well-being.

If you want your kids to appreciate what they have and who they are, give them a good example to follow – you. Practice being grateful for what you have by taking care of those things and people. Your kids will imitate you.

Practice gratitude to increase empathy and reduce aggression. Grateful people tend to be more sensitive and empathetic towards others. They are also less likely to retaliate or try to get revenge when provoked.

Learn to appreciate the trivial things in life. It can make you more resilient and can help you overcome trauma.

Productivity

Keep your mornings bright by tackling the time-consuming, boring, most disliked tasks at the end of the day.

Look at where you are spending your time; take inventory and make a list. You are sure to find areas in which you can improve.

When you find yourself procrastinating, ask yourself what is standing in your way. When you are aware, you can overcome the block and move forward.

Determine during which hours you are at peak performance. Do the most important tasks then.

Set clear, Smart achievable goals. Spend a few minutes each morning revisiting them.

Create a daily routine and stick to it. Long-term productivity is achieved through devotion.

If you struggle with self-discipline, find an accountability partner to hold you to your goals.

It is okay to say 'no.' If you are already pressed for time, do not volunteer to take on more duties. People appreciate it when you know your limits.

Stop multi-tasking. Studies suggest you get more accomplished when focusing on one task for several hours.

Take a 10-minute break for every 90 minutes you work. Walk, stretch, and drink some water during your break. This will help recharge your system.

Ask for help. Instead of struggling or procrastinating for hours, immediately ask for clarification or help. It can get you back on track in no time flat.

Clean out your email. Spend a few minutes each day cleaning out and organizing your email. Unsubscribe from newsletters you no longer read.

Some people work best on a short deadline. Others prefer to have a longer deadline and more time to deal with details. Organize your schedule and resources so you can get things done in either situation.

Confidence & Self-Esteem

Self-confidence comes from within. It really has nothing to do with what others think or say about you. But it has everything to do with what you think of yourself. Make sure what you think about yourself is not skewed by others.

Accept your achievements. Being humble and thankful is one thing but denying your achievements or thinking of them as a mistake is self-defeating. Learn to accept and even revel in your achievements.

Do not confuse feelings and facts. Feelings are fleeting and they will change. Just because you feel unworthy does not mean that you are unworthy. Keep things in perspective and remind yourself that this feeling will pass.

Thinking positive thoughts is great but you must also act on them. Actions make them real and give them more staying power. *Think positive. Act positive.*

Be aware of your self-talk. The minute you are aware of a negative thought, replace it with something positive. Do this throughout the day. Thinking positively will soon become a habit you can keep for a lifetime.

Accept your weakness and focus on your strengths. Perfection does not serve anyone.

Journal your thoughts. Analyse them to determine if your limitations are real or imagined.

The more goals you achieve, the more you train your brain to align itself with success.

Remember, failure does not define you. It simply means something did not work. Shrug it off and try again.

Surround yourself with confident, happy people. Mimic their actions until you feel it deep in your soul.

Prepare yourself. Consider what is the worst that can happen. Imagine how you will manage it. Now that you have envisioned the worst and know how to manage it, you can focus on doing your best.

Looking at your best elevates your self-esteem. To keep a youthful appearance, avoid using perfumes and lotions with added preservatives, which is known to speed up the aging process.

Empty generic affirmations do not help. For affirmations to work well, they must be believable and do-able. Affirmations should be positive, true facts about you. There must be something in the affirmation that you believe.

Build your self-esteem on facts. Identify your proven strengths and competencies. Gather the evidence or proof. Use the proof to bolster your self-esteem and confidence level.

Demonstrate your strengths and abilities by joining related groups and teams. Practice and focus on your strengths as much as possible. This helps you build a solid foundation of success and strengthens your body of "proof."

Learn to tolerate or accept positive feedback. Your ability to accept positive comments is important. Simply reply with, "Thank you." When you allow the positive in and outwardly react to feedback positively, you build self-esteem.

Allow yourself to feel pride, satisfaction, pleasure, related to your talents, skills, characteristics, accomplishments, etc. When you allow yourself to believe positive, proof-based things about yourself, you nourish your self-esteem.

Self-confidence is based on a belief in your competence, ability to learn and solve problems, as well as your self-worth. Nurture these three areas by developing each one and learning to believe in yourself.

Confidence is your belief in your ability to succeed. It is often a result of experiencing multiple successes. It is important to find balance in this area. Too much can result in unwise, risky choices. Too little can prevent you from trying.

Everyone wants social acceptance. They often try to please people. However, self-acceptance and appreciation are far more beneficial to your health and well-being. You cannot please everyone. You can please and accept yourself.

Everything new to you has a learning curve and is a challenge. Do not label efforts to learn with a "failure"" status because it is a process. Include an encouraging "not yet" status, indicating intention, determination, and hope.

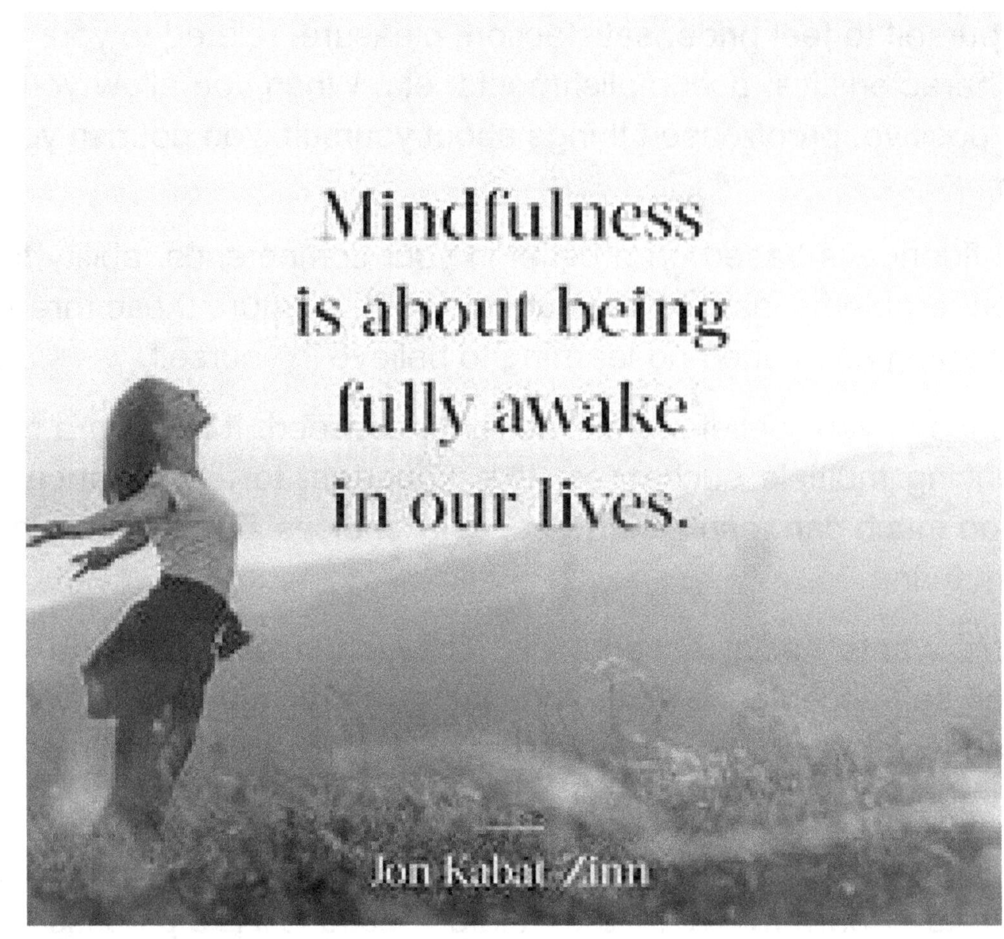

Mindfulness

Practice mindful breathing; in through your nose and out through your mouth. Focus your senses on the pathway of your breath.

Take time to be present in the moment. Let go of your thoughts and let your mind wander and explore your surroundings.

Instead of rushing through your daily routine, slow down and experience it fully. You will come away with greater understanding.

To experience life fully, you must engage your senses. Take time to experience your environment through each of your five senses. Focus on each sense one at a time.

Get with the program. Be mindful of the present. Instead of focusing on what is not, focus on what is.

Forgive yourself when you get distracted. It happens. Acknowledge your frustration then let it go. Most distractions will subside with practice.

Facing obstacles is part of life. See them as an opportunity to better yourself rather than something negative.

Concentration is the partner to mindfulness. Focus on developing your concentration and your mindfulness will improve.

At the end of each day, remind yourself of things you take for granted, a warm meal, a hot shower, a loving family, fragrant flowers, etc. Take a moment to appreciate them.

Study the people around you. Take in their voices, their differences, their similarities, and positive vibrations. Just be with them.

Pay attention to nature, it can teach you many things. Find a focal point in nature and visually explore every aspect of it. Then explore it with your other senses for a more vivid experience and understanding.

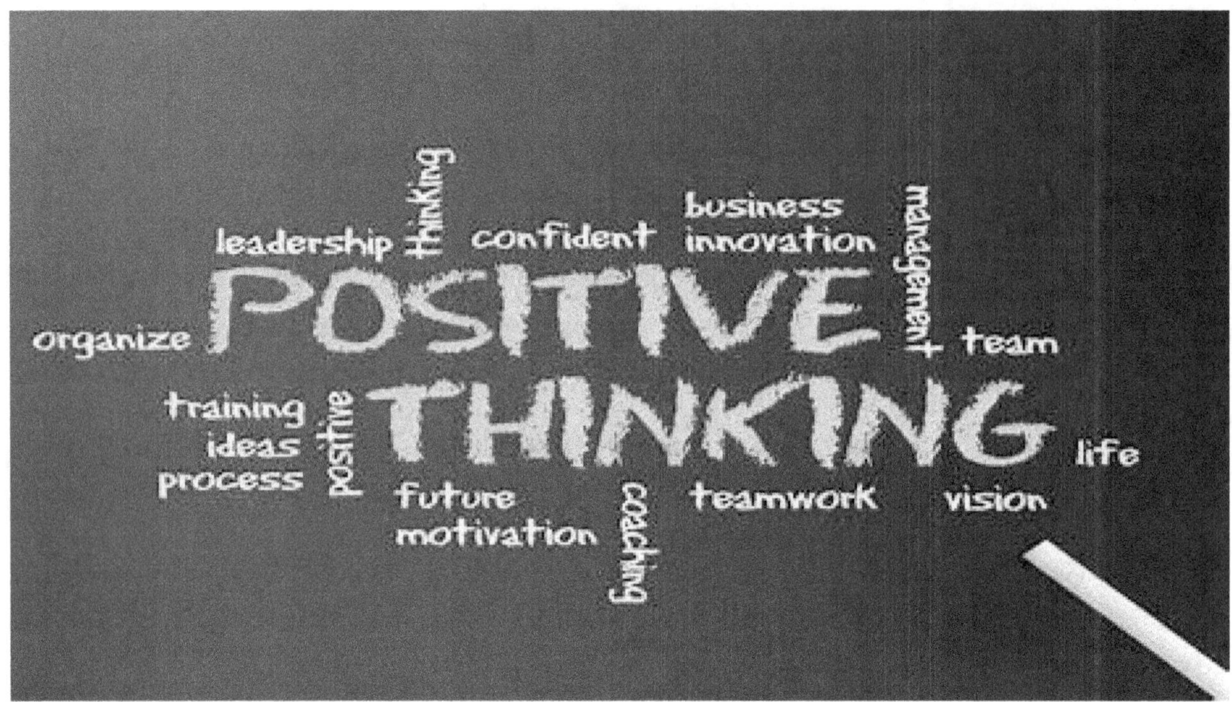

Positive Thinking

How you choose to start the morning sets the tone for the entire day. Start each day with a positive goal or compliment yourself on something specific.

When you surround yourself with positive people, you have little room for negative thoughts.

Spend time doing activities that are uplifting. Sing, dance, and enjoy the life you currently have.

Pay attention to your thoughts; if you are thinking negative thoughts, you are more likely to have negative experiences.

Take note of what you read as words have a direct impact on how you feel. The same is true of the words you speak. They can be powerful allies or destructive enemies.

Even during the most trying times, you can always find a little humour. Find it. Enjoy it. Remember it.

Stuff happens. You have the choice to dwell on the negative or turn it into a positive lesson.

Tune in to a different station. Be it music or TV, find an uplifting station and your mood will instantly improve.

Smile often. It releases endorphins and serotonin that make you feel better.

Set Smart goals for yourself. Celebrate when you meet one. No goal is too small to celebrate. No success is too small to encourage you.

Take responsibility for your life. You are not a victim. Stop making excuses. Having a better life starts with your decision to create it.

If you dread getting up in the morning, change your thought pattern and expectations. Expect and watch for something wonderful to happen.

Negative thought patterns can wreak havoc in your life. Interrupt the thoughts by breathing deeply or stretching when you catch them entering your mind.

Thinking positive thoughts can be immensely helpful and uplifting. However, if you couple your positive thinking with unrealistic, unobtainable, expectations. You will be disappointed in the outcome. Keep your expectations realistic.

Develop your positive, growth mindset with one word – 'Yet.' This small encouraging word is powerful. If you do not accomplish a goal when you want to, that does not mean you failed. You just have not succeeded…yet.

Research suggests thinking too positively about your success may decrease your motivation to work towards achieving your goal. Obviously, going overboard, even with positive thinking, can backfire.

When you envision your future success, make sure it is not a fantasized version. One study found that the most positive fantasies about the future predicted poor achievement. Do not confuse your fantasies with reality.

Improving your Memory

Listen to more instrumentals. Instrumental music has a positive impact on memory, focus, and attention.

Playing memory-improving "brain games" will keep your mind feeling fit.

Activities such as photography, painting, knitting, woodworking, and drawing are great brain exercises.

Want to improve your memory? Pay attention. You cannot remember what your brain failed to process.

Get creative. Write a fiction story, a song, or a poem. Use pen and paper instead of electronics to give your brain an extra boost of memory-staying power.

To improve memory, eat brain-enhancing foods such as avocado, fresh berries, cold-water fish, fermented foods and those high in omega-3 and vitamins C, K, E and B.

Learn a new skill. Continued learning ensures your neural connections stay active and strong. Never stop learning. And try learning something new every day.

Exercise improves blood flow and stimulates nerve cells, ensuring your memory stays strong and healthy.

Maintain your memory through hydration. Studies suggest that as little as 2% dehydration can affect your memory, attention, and other cognitive skills.

To keep your mind sharp, give it time to "rest" and process the day's events. Try to get at least 7 hours of sleep a night.

Science suggests it takes 8 seconds to move facts from short-term memory to long-term memory. When trying to remember vital details, focus on them for a minimum of 8 seconds.

Read more. Keeping yourself engaged intellectually is a great memory booster and keeps you up to date on the latest.

Learn to speak a new language. Even knowing a few words and phrases of a non-native language is enough to improve your memory.

Consider learning your favourite song in a different language. You already know the native words and tunes. Your brain will work to help you "translate" it. When you combine these two memory boosters, it is more fun and beneficial.

Play concentration. Using regular cards (or fun cards for kids) play a few rounds of concentration. Look at each "face-up" card for 8-10 seconds. Play as usual. This helps you strengthen your memory skills using familiar images.

Play board games that require moving a game piece and counting the spaces. This helps to strengthen short-term memory.

Play "Connect Four" or similar strategy-based games. When you survey the playing board carefully and count, it strengthens logic and memory skills.

Calming the Mind

Use all your senses. Each of the senses – sight, hearing, smell, touch, and taste, affect a different part of your brain. Use all your senses to reach multiple areas and receive a deeper sense of calm.

When your mind seems like an eight-lane highway at rush hour, close some of those lanes and reduce the speed.

Rev up your endorphins, are hormones your body releases to counteract pain, sadness, tension, anger, in addition to other negative emotions and thoughts. Movement is the key to increasing endorphin levels, which gives you feelings of pleasure, satisfaction, as well as a calmer, positive, and more focused mind.

Use essential oils such as lavender, jasmine, or sandalwood in your home to induce a calming peaceful effect. They not only smell good and may have natural calming properties, but they can trigger good memories associated with the scents.

Eat slowly and concentrate on the experience. When you eat too fast, you are not able to enjoy or savour the experience. The calming aromas, flavours, and textures of the food are lost when you scarf your food down quickly.

Act with intention. When you listen, speak, and think with intention, your mind will slow down, focus on the purpose of the activity, and filter out distractions.

Take a catnap. If you can, a 15-minute nap will rejuvenate your mind and help to calm you down.

Practice emotional freedom tapping (EFT). This mind-body tapping technique is a wonderful way to regain balance in your life, as you neutralize negative thoughts and emotions, which hold you back.

Take a hot bath or shower to calm your mind. Hot water soothes your mind and relaxes your muscles.

Practice mindful breathing. Mindful breathing helps you to slow your racing mind and reconnect with yourself.

Be present in your surroundings. Sometimes, we get stuck inside our heads. Pay attention to what is really in front of you.

Find and Create Happiness

Look at pictures of happy, smiling people. Smiles are contagious. This subliminal suggestion works, especially when combined with humour.

Turn up the volume on tunes that make feel happy, bring back good memories, or make you want to move to the music. It will make you feel better.

Make a conscious effort to think positively throughout the day. It will increase your happiness quotient, which will also help you ignore negative comments and dramatics.

Practice gratitude every day. Express your appreciation by giving to and supporting others. Not only does this make you and others happy but it helps you keep things in perspective. Like smiles, gratitude is contagious. Pass your happiness around.

Give heart-felt compliments. When you compliment others and make them feel good, your hormones kick in and make you feel wanted, needed, and happy.

Smile even when you do not feel like it. Your brain notices what your muscles do, and it responds in specific ways. When you smile, regardless of the reason, your brain goes into happy mode and often changes a bad mood into a happier one.

Do something nice for someone. When you do something nice for someone, you feel good about yourself and the other person.

Say thank you to someone for something they did. Everyone wants to be appreciated but people often neglect to acknowledge others' efforts. Make someone feel happy and your own happiness level will increase in the process.

Recall old, fond memories. Memories are a fantastic way to relive and remember happy times, especially after someone passes away or moves out of your life.

Allow yourself to be silly or more child-like. Hop in a swing, colour a picture, jump rope, or something else you did in your childhood. If possible, do these things with a close friend or a child in your life to share the happiness. *Just have fun!*

Volunteer to do something for a favourite cause or organization. You want to be needed and matter or have influence in the world. Volunteering enables you to use your special talents and gifts to make others happier and, in the process, make the world a better place.

Learn to enjoy the trivial things in life and everything else will seem to be grand, by comparison.

If you could use a regular dose of happiness for a while, stock up on curry, chilies, or other hot peppers such as cayenne. These trigger your endorphins, which make you feel good and well balanced.

Giving and Receiving Forgiveness

Choose to forgive yourself and others. Anger, resentment, shame, and guilt are among the strong emotions that can have a negative effect on your life. Forgive and make room for happiness, satisfaction, confidence and more.

When you forgive someone, you make a choice to free yourself from a past transgression or event. You no longer give an incident undeserved priority in your life, and you are better able to move on in a happier, more fulfilling life.

Grudges are heavy. Carrying a grudge, especially long-term, can make you emotionally tired, cranky, and bitter, among other things. Stop hauling that baggage around by forgiving yourself and others.

Refusing to forgive enables you to relive the negative emotions repeatedly, which inhibits your ability to prosper. Let go of the pain and resentment as you forgive.

Give your life a thorough spring-cleaning. Detox your mind, identify, and acknowledge your hurt feelings. Forgive those responsible, let the feelings go, and make room for joy and abundance.

We have all said or done something that hurt someone. When you realize and acknowledge this, take responsibility. Own up to it, ask for forgiveness, and make amends when possible.

Forgiving does not mean the people who hurt your feelings are right or justified in what they said or did. It means you choose to stop giving the incident power in the present and in the future.

Forgiveness is not guaranteed. When you ask for forgiveness, you may not receive it immediately or ever. Do your part to make amends. You cannot control how someone else feels or what they think. Move on and do not repeat the mistake or deed.

Forgiving someone does not mean you pretend that something did not hurt or happened. It means you let go of the past pain because you cannot change what happened. You can only change your own actions and attitudes in the present.

Remember a time when you made a poor choice, were insensitive, acted selfishly, acted based on a mistaken belief, lashed out at someone out of pain, and did something embarrassing. When you understand yourself and your motives, it is easier to forgive yourself, as well as others.

You may need to forgive or receive forgiveness from someone that is no longer in your life. Consider writing a letter to the person. Burn the letter. Envision your pain and negative feelings floating away with the smoke. Message sent and received – forgiven.

Self-Love Principles

Give yourself the same loving care, attention, and sound advice you give to others, using self-talk. Keep self-talks positive, encouraging, and fact based. Not only will this help you to focus on the positive, but it will also enable you to help others better.

We tend to expect more from ourselves than we do from others. Forgive yourself just as you forgive others who make mistakes. Acknowledge, accept, and forgive.

Let go of feelings, situations, and people that do not support your best interests. Riding your life of these makes room for more positive, goal-supporting influences.

Make self-care time a top priority. You are available to meet others' needs and wants. Do the same for yourself. Your needs and wants are just as important, even more so. If your needs go unmet, you cannot effectively help others.

Practice little acts of self-love throughout the day. Take extra time to care for yourself. Congratulate yourself on a job done well. Do things you enjoy. These little gifts reinforce your self-worth, confidence, self-esteem, and more.

Never confuse self-love with selfishness. Showing respect for your personal wants and needs is not selfish. When you do not love and respect yourself, it is difficult to give and accept those things from others. Do everyone a favour. Learn how to respect and love yourself.

Love yourself the same way you love other people. Be available for yourself. Forgive your mistakes. Set boundaries. Respect your limitations. Make your expectations realistic. Acknowledge achievements. Work on goals.

Beating yourself up never helps. In fact, continuing to chastise yourself can lead to a bad habit of being overly critical of yourself and others. Consider mistakes a learning opportunity. Practice and share the lessons you learn.

Accept and love yourself, just as you are. You are a work in progress. Nobody, not even you, should expect perfection. Instead, work towards improvement.

While the term, self-love, might seem like an easy decision, many people do not know how to accept, respect, and love themselves. This is essential to maintaining peace, happiness, and a balanced life.

When you begin to love yourself, you also start to feel worthy. This comes across to others. You may find that more people feel drawn to you. Build healthy connections and relationships for a more fulfilling and enjoyable life.

Be honest with yourself. Denying the truth just because it is not what you want is a form of self-disrespect. Show your self-respect by trusting that you will accept the facts with grace and make the best of things.

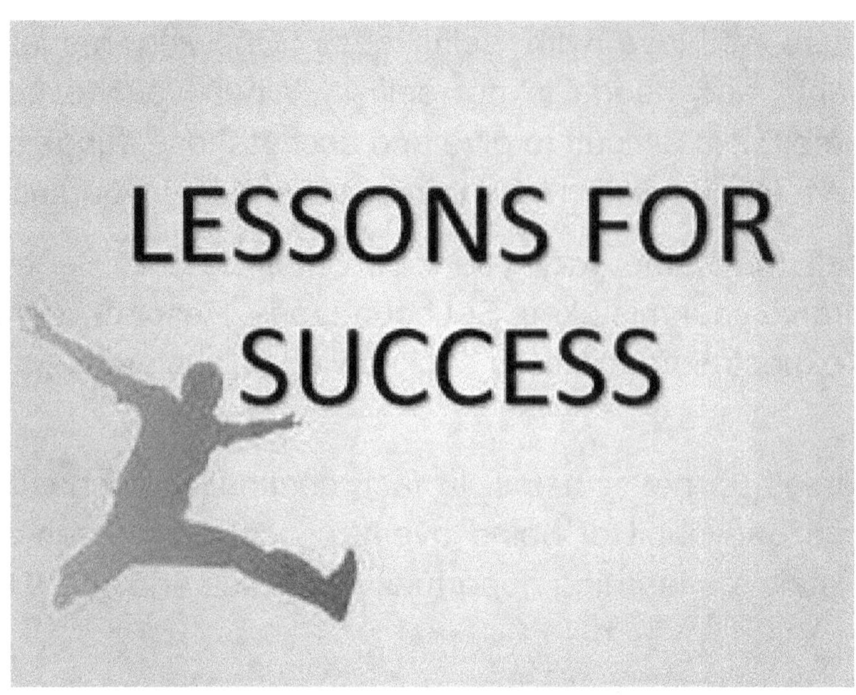

Lessons for Success

Divide complex goals into smaller, attainable subsets. This increases your success rate, which gives you confidence and encouragement to continue in other areas.

Reward yourself after you achieve a goal. For maximum effect, the reward should relate to the goal in some way. This motivates you to keep working towards specific goals and overall success.

Celebrate even small successes. No achievement is too small. This is especially helpful in the beginning. You need to build one success on the back of a previous success to elevate your confidence.

Start talking about your goals. The more excited you are, the more excited others will be. This excitement can quickly lead to others following you to reach your level of success.

Build your integrity with others by being honest and true to your word. When you promise something, follow through on it. If you do not, your reputation and success will suffer the consequences.

Focus on what you want to achieve in life. Plan daily steps to make it a reality. Even if you need to backtrack or take a different route, you are still moving towards your goal. With each step, you are closer to success.

You cannot succeed if you do not try repeatedly. Most successes are not due to luck. They are a product of hard work, perseverance, and a determination to reach a specific goal.

Do not take the words of naysayers to heart. Some people are just "negative nellies" and have little to say that is positive, encouraging, or could be seen as constructive criticism. Your success depends on what you believe and do.

Allow yourself the time and room to make mistakes. Those mistakes are the stepping-stones that will lead to your success. Just apply the valuable lessons you learn from your experiences.

Success means different things to different people. Define, in detail, what you consider "success" to be. Describe how you will recognize it. Unless you know exactly what you are aiming for, you will never be successful.

Success does not always come in traditional ways. Your version of success will be as unique as it is. It will also depend on what you do and how you do it. But mostly, it will depend on how you measure "success." Measure carefully.

Many people equate success with money. However, for most people success is related to overcoming personal obstacles and achieving goals. There are many kinds of successes. Do not limit yourself to one definition of the term.

Take small steps every day toward your goal. One day, you will look up and realize you have succeeded. Apply what you learned to obtain success in another area of your life.

If you fail initially, make needed changes, and keep moving forward. You cannot reach success ahead of you continually turn around to focus on the past.

Success comes from being honest with yourself and others. You cannot reach any level of true success through short cuts or trickery, which compromise your integrity. Honesty and integrity form the foundation of success.

If you focus on your strengths, your weaknesses will seem small by comparison. However, if you accept your strengths and focus on developing weak areas into strengths, you will have a greater chance of succeeding.

Your mindset plays a key role in your life. If you have developed a growth mindset, you are more likely to continue working hard despite setbacks. This mindset helps you to grow, achieve goals and succeed.

Health Improvement

Being healthy includes each of the parts that make you unique - your body, mind, emotions, and spirit. Each part contributes to your overall health so make sure you do something to strengthen each part, daily.

A good night's sleep is as vital as a healthy diet to your health. Take steps to ensure you get a good night's rest.

Drinking plenty of water is essential to having a clear mind. We are made up mostly of water. It makes sense to replenish what we use. Staying hydrated helps you to feel your best.

Even with the healthiest diet, it is important to take supplements. Supplements pick up where your diet leaves off. This ensures you get all your daily requirements.

Plenty of sunshine is vital for optimal health. If you cannot get enough sunshine, have your vitamin D checked. If you are lacking, you might need to supplement.

When beginning an exercise program, include a plan for indoor exercising. DVD exercise programs are a wonderful way to vary the type of exercise you do. Get a good DVD for each type of exercise - aerobics, strength, balance, and flexibility.

Exercise at least three times per week for 30 minutes each time. Even if you must go to bed a little later or rise a few minutes earlier, it is essential to your overall health.

Eat your broccoli. If you have heard your parents, tell you to eat your broccoli, they will love you a lot. Broccoli is chock full of nutrients but also has cancer-fighting properties.

Hate to exercise? Commit to exercising every day for 15-minutes or more, without fail. Vary the type of exercise, the location, and/or the time you start to keep you motivated and moving. Make exercising an easy habit to form.

Make the rounds and circulate. Sitting or standing in the same spot for a prolonged period is not good for your circulation. Make it a point to get up and walk around for a quick energy boost and to help your circulation. Move it or lose it.

The later in the day it gets, the less you should eat. Eat a big breakfast, a medium lunch, and a small, light dinner. Avoid after dinner snacks or eating before bed.

Satisfy your hunger with flavourful foods. Some diets and dishes consist of bland foods and ingredients. This can lead to eating more as you try to satisfy your hunger. Add flavourful spices without adding calories.

If you prefer flavourful meat while on a diet, consider adding mustard, salsa, Worcestershire sauce, flavoured vinegar, teriyaki sauce, or spicy sauce. These add flavours without adding calories. Make sure they are allowed on your diet.

Before you pay for your meds at the pharmacy, open the bag. Make sure it is yours and everything is correct. Mistakes are easily made, and you do not want to take the wrong medicine or dose. Doing so could be fatal.

Age is just a number. Studies show that if you act old, you will feel old. But that is not the worst part. You can end up developing or suffering from problems before your time. Think young, act young (within reason), have fun, and feel young.

Watch your mouth! Gum disease and heart disease go hand in hand. Up to 91% of patients have both diseases. Some believe there is a direct connection between the two. Make dental care a top priority to maintain physical health.

When fitness is a priority, take what your scales say with a grain of salt. Regular bathroom scales only measure total weight. They do not measure overall fitness or body fat. Talk with your doctor about BMI (body mass index.)

Fidget more for better health. Studies show fidgeting increases blood flow and circulation while sitting. Tap your toes, twitch your foot, bounce your leg, and fidget more. Walking is better but fidgeting is good for your health.

Well-being

A sense of well-being does not come from doing any one thing: it is all about balance. Balance all areas of your life, and you will have a heightened sense of well-being.

Improve your sense of well-being by learning a new skill. The sense of adventure and accomplishment when you master a new skill adds to your overall confidence and optimism.

Food has a tremendous impact on your feelings and emotions. If you are feeling down, reach for some omega-3 rich foods (fish, nuts, and seeds) to lift and balance your outlook.

Do not forget about your inner child. Being a grownup is hard. Play or do something silly, occasionally, to honour your inner child's needs.

To feel your best, you need to rest and relax. Take short breaks during the day to refocus and relax your mind. Breathing exercises or meditation for a minute or two to centre yourself and regain your mind-body balance.

Laugh and smile for a quick pick me up. When you laugh, play, and have fun, your feel-good hormones quickly elevate your sense of well-being.

Be available for real-life, personal connections. Interacting with others, in person, helps you relate to the world around you, heightens your sense of connection, and gives you a feeling of well-being.

Feeling out of sorts? Give to others and watch the magic begin. Contributing to your community or to a cause increases your sense of value and gives you the feeling that everything will be okay.

Take needed breaks. When something is frustrating or you cannot collect your thoughts, taking a break allows your mind to balance and sort things out in the background. When you go back to the task, it is easier to complete.

Do not be afraid to delegate. Getting help is not a sign of weakness. Delegating tasks to others allows you to balance your workload. It is very freeing.

Learn to say 'no.' Being able to say 'no' when you need to give yourself control over situations. Your ability to control what you do and when you do it allows you to maintain balance and is good for your overall sense of well-being.

Live out your personal values and ethics. When you act on what you believe, you will develop a sense of balance, confidence, and fulfilment.

Sometimes you may feel that you spend most of your time doing things for other people. Take time every morning to do something you enjoy. This will ensure that more of your needs are met, and you get a feeling of well-being.

Relationships

The most important relationship you have is the one you have with *yourself*. When you know and love yourself, it draws others to you and makes those healthy relationships more meaningful.

Lasting relationships require good communications. Develop your speaking and listening skills to deepen the connection of any relationship.

Improve your relationships by accepting that everyone is different and has their own individual needs. These needs may take them on different journeys and down different paths in life. Celebrate individualism in relationships.

Healthy relationships start with an open heart. Accept people, as they are --faults and all. This includes accepting yourself. This helps you develop healthy relationships and realistic expectations.

Never stop learning and growing on an individual, personal level. Your relationships will thrive when everyone's needs are met, and you find a common middle ground. Balance individual and group needs for best results.

If you want solid relationships, become more interesting. When you have a large variety of interests, you have more to share. This variety of interests attracts like-minded people and forms the basis of a solid relationship.

Make friends and partners feel important. Check in for no reason. Reach out to say 'hi.' Leave a special note or send a text to re-connect. These gestures show your loved ones that they matter and are important to you.

When in a relationship, people should have individual space as well as together time. Two individuals can equal one happy couple when both individual and couple needs are balanced.

Just as you support each other's "me-time," support togetherness time by setting a date night to reconnect. This allows you to grow as individuals and as a couple, while strengthening your relationship.

Take some time to play and have fun in your relationship. Whether it is a friendship or a partnership, plan time to laugh and have fun. Fond memories and shared experiences deepen your bond and encourage repeats.

Talk with your partner before making a decision that affects them. Skipping this step makes your partner feel that they do not matter. Always give your partner a say in what happens to them and build a trusting, safe environment.

People come in and out of your life. Appreciate and let go of those who need to leave and cherish the ones who stay.

Make confidentiality one of your top 3 priorities. People you are close to trust you. If you betray that trust, by blabbing about a private matter, the relationship will be damaged. Make a special effort to keep private conversations private.

Friendships are especially important to every individual. Even if you have a romantic relationship, you also need friends. One person cannot meet all your needs or share all your interests. Encourage others to have multiple friendships.

Be available to spend time with the people you care about. It is true that spending time with loved ones is the best gift you can give. Show them you care by making them a top priority in your life. Spend time with them regularly.

Do not tolerate or make excuses for disrespect, deception, manipulation, or any kind of abuse – verbal, mental, emotional, or physical. This applies to every type of relationship. If you want to try and work things out, do it from a safe distance.

Be respectful of your friend or partner's need for time alone. Everyone deals with disappointment, stress, and grief differently. Tell them that you are there when they are ready to talk. When they work through things, they will come to you.

Communication

Pay attention to body language to get the full message that is being sent. The subliminal messages can give you a "feeling" that something is not right. Trust your feelings and intuition. Keep your eyes open to communicate well.

Listening, rather than hearing, is important to effective communication. Listen more and interrupt less to make people feel that they matter, and they have been heard. This skill can be helpful in every aspect of your life. Use it often.

When you have something to say, be clear and concise. Nobody enjoys hearing someone beat around the bush. They will appreciate and respect you for it. Getting to the point quickly helps to avoid misunderstandings.

Giving the right amount and type of eye contact is important when communicating. Eye contact should be genuine and gentle. Avoid intense stares. These make people uncomfortable, and they shut down.

Unless you are approachable, people do not try to talk with you. To be more approachable, smile and make eye contact. Your body language should be open and inviting. These things invite others to talk and connect with you.

Communication is about mutual sharing. If you find yourself focusing on yourself, turn that around and focus on others by asking a question. It takes the pressure off, and everyone likes to share their experiences.

Be friendly when meeting people. When it comes to communicating effectively, the friendlier you are, the easier it is to foster a new relationship.

Remember that everybody is different. Keep in mind that each person has different tastes and opinions. Sharing similarities and differences makes for interesting conversations and enjoyable learning opportunities.

If you want to make a good impression, mirror the other person a bit. For example, match their head tilt once or twice. This fosters a feeling of connectedness and may suggest that you are both on the same page.

A group meeting does not have to be an all-day event. A quick check-in twice a week may be all your group needs to keep them on track and motivated. This works well for most groups, including church, school, and social groups.

Choose the right form of communication. Sometimes texts and emails are misunderstood. Follow up with verbal communication. This gives you a chance to verify receipt as well as clarify or expand on a subject.

Healthy Socializing

Sometimes new social situations can be awkward. You can help alleviate this feeling by breaking the ice and making the other person more comfortable. Begin with a common interest or find one to create a relaxed mood.

To connect socially, join a group of interest or explore new options. There are local, regional, and worldwide fan clubs for every interest or hobby. Facebook is a suitable place to start your search and find other groups.

The best social advice of the century is to put down the phone. Not only is it rude to look at your phone while talking with someone, but it is the perfect way to disconnect from the relationship. Turn off the phone to really connect.

Your passions, interests, and experiences give you loads of things to share in social groups. Find groups where you feel comfortable. Participate often to make more connections.

After joining a few groups, consider creating an event of your own. Instead of sitting around waiting to be invited to a great party, host one and meet more like-minded people.

Let people know about a group or event by sending them invitations. Be sure to include a "personal" message when possible. Also, encourage them to pass along the info to other friends. Events are more fun when shared with a friend.

If you want a healthy social life, try something new. Trying new things makes your life more interesting. It also broadens your skills and knowledge. These make you more attractive to others so get out there and try something new.

Expand your circle. If you need a change, start a new hobby, and join a related club or group. It is okay to make new friends and spend some time with them. Just do not neglect your other friends. You can have them both.

Tired of the status quo? Grab a few friends and attend a local event, try out a new restaurant, join a local club, get involved in a community project, etc. Getting out and doing more expands your opportunities to meet people.

Take some time to explore the art of small talk. Small talk can seem flat and boring, but if you practice the art of small talk, you can make it fun. Keep in mind that small talk often leads to more personal talks and relationships.

Include your pets in your social life. Many restaurants, cafes, other businesses, and parks welcome your fur-babies. Take your pet, when possible, they are great icebreakers and help to lighten the mood with their antics.

HOW TO GET
MORE ENERGY

1. Get more sleep.
2. Get high-quality sleep.
3. Reduce your carbohydrate intake.
4. Avoid eating junk food.
5. Use adaptogenic herbs.
6. Drink vegetable juice.
7. Stay hydrated.
8. Eat chia seeds.
9. Drink herbal teas.
10. Take B vitamins.
11. Address psychological issues that make you lethargic.
12. Exercise.
13. Try essential oils.
14. Stop bad habits.
15. Avoid burnouts.
16. Be social.
17. Do yoga

Improving Energy

If you want to increase your energy, take a few minutes throughout the day to do the "Yogic Coffee" breathing exercise. This 30 second to 2-minute exercise combines cardiovascular and breathing to give you a quick energy and oxygen boost during the day. https://www.youtube.com/watch?v=NH0ZdkGSAPU

Walk it off. When feeling lethargic, take a brisk walk. Even ten minutes can increase your endorphins as well as your oxygen and energy levels.

When it comes to increasing your energy, eat small snacks throughout the day. A few nuts or a piece of fruit will energize your brain quickly because it does not have an energy reserve and needs a steady supply of nutrients.

Staying hydrated is particularly important to your energy level. If you are not a huge fan of water, try adding some lemon or lime. The water helps to carry energizing nutrients and oxygen through your body so find a way to drink more water.

If you feel sluggish, turn up the music and dance it off. A few minutes of dancing around can raise your heart rate and oxygen level, while increasing your energy level. The music can also give you an extra lift.

Take an "almost" nap. Sometimes all you need to regain your energy is to close your eyes and relax for a few minutes. Powernaps can work wonders, especially when you do not have time to take a real nap.

Laugh it off. Use humour to boost your energy and mood. Read, watch, or listen to something funny. Laughing aloud can give you the energy you need to continue your task, refreshed and revitalized.

To boost your energy at work, surround yourself with items that are *red, orange, or yellow.* Look at these items when you feel sleepy, tired, or low on energy. Consider using a computer that has a yellow or orange casing/cover.

Take a mindful break. Take a moment to become present to all your surroundings and focus on what is in front of you. This is great practice to focus on what is and forget about being tired.

Take a 10-minute vacation. Close your eyes, breathe deeply, and imagine your vacation spot in detail. Imagine the scents, sounds, feel of textures, tastes, and visuals. Open your eyes to a refreshed and energized you.

Rest and Sleep

We have all heard that 8 hours of sleep is essential to being productive. Take inventory of your sleep habits and see what you need to change and improve. An actual list of your sleep habits on paper is a real revelation.

One hour before bed, stop using visual electronics. These tend to stimulate your brain, making it difficult to relax.

Slip in some quiet time before bed and unplug from social media. Try reading your favourite book instead.

As the night unfolds, you should become more relaxed and not in a get-it-done before bedtime frenzy. Stick to time schedules to make sure things are done and everyone has settled in 1-2 hours before their bedtime.

Make it routine to incorporate calming practices such as prayer, meditation, or yoga an hour before bed. This new habit will relax you and help you sleep better.

If you wake up in the middle of the night and cannot fall back to sleep, try changing rooms, lowering the heat, doing deep breathing and meditation.

If you can manage a short nap during your day in a safe environment on your lunch hour, see if this practice recharges your battery.

Feeling sleepy and cannot seem to re-energize? Try a power walk for 10 minutes during your lunch hour.

If you are not getting the proper amount of sleep and feel groggy during the day, try using all-natural supplements at night to help you reset the clock.

The foods you eat will have a significant impact on the quality of your sleep. If you eat too much sugar before bed, do not scratch your head and wonder why you cannot sleep.

Practice tensing and relaxing your muscles before bed to learn the difference between being relaxed and being stressed.

Mental Health

Journal to get problems and worries off your mind and make room for positive, productive thoughts.

For a quick mental lift, there is nothing like a breath of fresh air. Get out and get some air. If you cannot get out, open a window or door to bring the fresh air in. The change of scenery as well as the scent helps you to reset your mind.

There is nothing like having a friendly conversation to boost your mood. Talk with a positive person. Not only does positivity help but so does the one-on-one interaction.

For an instant mental boost, listen to some upbeat music. Listening to music activates every part of your brain so start creating more playlists for better brain function, mood management, and mental health.

Get a dose (or five) of laughter each day. It helps to maintain mental health, elevate your mood, and much more. Laughter gives your whole brain a "mental" workout. So, make sure you take time to laugh frequently.

Exercise is a perfect way to get into a better frame of mind. Fire up those endorphins to power up your positive thought process.

For better mental health and brain function, spice up your recipes with cloves, cinnamon, nutmeg, and other spices. Research discovered that these provide nutrients, which sharpen memory, reduce stress, and improve sleep.

If you need a mental boost, spend time with your funniest friend. Good belly laughs are an instant mental pick me up. The effects tend to last well after you have stopped laughing since your mind replays the memory.

Eat dark chocolate to lighten your load and lift your mood. Dark chocolate is one of the few food sources for anandamide, a neurotransmitter that is also known as the "bliss molecule."

Want a quick mental pick me up? Look at pleasing pictures of favourite holiday destinations. The visuals will help your brain focus on the positive, pleasurable aspects of life.

Managing Emotional Health

If you feel emotionally disconnected, take some time to reconnect with supportive friends and family. Talking with these people is a surefire way to regain that sense of connection. Make it a habit to contact them more often.

Manage your emotions with memories. Create positive memories with people you care about. When your emotions are out of control, pull out a memory to help you regain emotional balance and put things in perspective.

The best cure for "poor me" feeling is to volunteer. When you concentrate on the needs of others or doing a good deed, your focus shifts away from yourself.

If you feel you are in a slump, add something new into the mix. Choose something that motivates, inspires, excites, educates, fascinates, or interests you. It can be anything from getting a new book to learning something new to do.

If you feel bad about something in your life, it could be time to teach someone something new. Whether it is as a tutor or a sports coach, teaching someone else something takes your mind off your troubles.

Join a group if you are feeling out of sorts emotionally. Whether it is a support group or a book group, this can lift your emotional health.

Everyone gets stressed and worried. Learning to let go of the things you have no control over is the best way to manage stress and all the emotions that go along with it. If you cannot fix something, boot the thoughts out of your mind.

Control your emotions/feelings. Smile, even if you do not want to. Meditate to refocus. Wait 90 seconds for the feeling to dissipate. Do something you love. All of this helps you control your feelings. Practice, practice, practice.

Use good memories to change your mood. Pair a good memory with a tangible object -- a vacation and seashells or flowers. To get on track, bring out one of the objects for a few days. Use your senses to remember and re-focus.

Emotional eating can wreak havoc on your mind and body. Use other ways to get that "feel-good" boost. If you feel angry or hurt, walk, run, or act out "throwing" the feeling out of your system. Moving quickly gives you a boost.

Create an emo pack filled with healthy snacks and other items that help you to manage your emotions. This is especially helpful if you put it in the car for an unforeseen issue or need an extra boost.

Playing with your pets provides fun and laughter. It also reminds you that you are loved, unconditionally, and that you are wanted and needed. Spend more time with your pet, especially when you are going through a rough spot.

Improve Physical Health

Physical health includes every part of your body, from your hair to the nail on your little toe and everything in between. Care for each part to ensure that your overall physical health is the best it can be.

Your hair often mirrors your overall health. It can reveal nutritional issues, problems with organs, infections, excessive stress, menopause onset, a dangerous diet, and more. Pay more attention to your hair to see the signs.

Healthy hair requires healthy foods. Make sure you get your daily amount of iron, zinc, vitamins (A, B, C, and D) as well as protein, omega-3, folate, and biotin. When you take care of your hair, your whole-body benefits.

The 'eyes' have it. Part of keeping your eyes healthy involves knowing your family's eye history. When you know certain conditions and diseases exist, your doctors know to watch those closely.

Protect your eyes from UV rays and accidents. Wear sunglasses that block 100% of UV-A and UV-B rays. Use protective glasses when playing sports or working around the home. Once your eyesight is lost, it will not return.

Hearing loss is a common health problem in the U.S. If it is hard to hear normal speaking volumes or crowd chatter sounds garbled, talk with your doctor. The cause may be something minor or serious. Get help before it is too late.

Some 200+ medicines can affect hearing and balance. Among them are aspirin, antibiotics, diuretics, and other common medications. Always read the side effects and directions, even if it is not a new med. Know the signs.

Skin is your natural suite of armour, protecting you 24/7. However, any chink in the armour makes it less effective. Take care of your skin so it will continue to protect you throughout your entire life. This is especially important for kids.

Protect your skin year-round. Clean and moisturize it daily. Use UV-A and UV-B blocking sunscreen in every season, whether it is cloudy or sunny. UV rays are always present. Make a habit of protecting your skin for better health.

Diabetic dry skin. Dry skin is less resilient and is easily damaged. If you have diabetes, moisturize, and protect your skin from even the smallest nick. These make you more susceptible to dangerous infections.

Read your nails. Your nails often signal when something is wrong in your body. Care for your nails and learn what is normal. Report changes in colour, texture, thickness, splitting, and rippling. These indicate something is wrong.

If you do not like exercise, think of it as simply moving. Raise your arms, reach for things, walk outside, etc. Regardless of what you call it, moving gives your body a tune-up. Move more for better physical health.

Make it a goal to take more steps each day. Use a step-counter to help you. Write the total down each day. This helps you track your progress, challenge yourself, and succeed.

Create a daily activity/exercise routine and stick to it. It can include housework, taking a special walk, inviting a friend or group over to exercise with you or anything else you want. The key is to make it a routine, so it becomes a habit.

Exercising is more fun with company. Grab a friend or your pet and get moving. Adding an element of fun often allows you to exercise longer without noticing the time or getting tired as quickly.

Spiritual

Want to contact your inner spirit? Check your core values. Evaluating your values helps you to define and refine your spiritual beliefs.

Trying to be spiritual in a human world can be challenging. Make your spiritual practices a top priority so you can stick to your beliefs even when tempted to do otherwise.

Create time for spiritual practices daily. Daily spiritual activities help you to keep your beliefs in focus.

To keep your spiritual life in order, surround yourself with like-minded people. They will encourage and support you when you get confused or need help.

Spiritual health can lead to physical wealth. Focus on what you believe to be true, good, and fair. A strong belief system can be very uplifting and healthy.

If you want spiritual health, express yourself. Speak the truth or journal your thoughts.

Explore the deeper meaning of your life. You never know what you may uncover. The more you explore, the more you will understand and love yourself.

If you want to find peace in your world, you must start with yourself. When you can accept that you are not in control of anything but yourself, your faith in a higher power can help to bring you peace.

Keep a "thankful/grateful" journal to help you count and remember your blessings. During tough times, these can encourage you and put things into perspective.

Spiritual wellness includes your values. If you have made decisions that do not align with your values, you may feel uncomfortable or out of sorts. Make it a habit to examine your values before you make decisions and take actions.

Talk with people who do not believe as you do. When you talk with these people, you listen and try to understand their point of view. This helps you to discover the path that is right for you.

Nurture a healthy spirit with purposeful practices such as making it a point to act with compassion and acceptance. When you purposely focus on the practice, your spiritual strength and health increases.

Walk a spiritual labyrinth. Labyrinths can be found in many areas from small towns to large cities. These allow you to move, meditate, and contemplate at the same time. This whole-body activity helps to connect every part of you.

Colour me impressed. Consider using *colouring mandalas* to connect with your spirit, tap into your creativity, and relax. The circle represents wholeness, unity, harmony and more. This helps you to focus on your spiritual wholeness.

MONEY MANAGEMENT TIPS

CONTROL EXPENSES
Save at least 10% of earnings & pay the most important person first

PAY DOWN BAD DEBT
Includes credit cards & personal loans. Investment debt is tax-deductible and good

DIVERSIFY INVESTMENTS
Cash and term deposits are safe but historically underperform property and shares

RESEARCH BEFORE INVESTING
Do not invest based on speculation and ideas that are too good to be true

INVEST FOR THE LONG TERM
But review your portfolio semi-annually or yearly

REDUCE YOUR STRESS
Consult a professional financial planner

Saving, Making, and Managing Money

Saving money is a big part of making money. Learn to save your money and you will not feel the continual need to work longer and longer hours to get things that you do not really want or need.

Hit the clearance racks first. You can save quite a bit of money when you snap up these great deals at the end of each season. Many holiday sales re-offer the picked-through "leftovers" from the seasonal sales.

Buy in bulk. Get a friend or two to do this with you. When you make bulk buying a team effort, you can get better deals, and you do not need a huge storage area to house all your goodies.

Use coupons to save as much as possible. This is easy with digital and store coupons. Sign up with your favourite stores to get advance notice of sales to save even more. Be sure to follow the instructions and read the details.

Buy store or generic brands. Some brand name company's produce store brand items. These are cheaper, yet are the same quality, and flavour. Use store coupons with these for extra savings.

Do not just work to earn a living, work to create a rewarding life. While we all need money, when you work to have a rewarding and happy life, you are more likely to meet your goals and be successful.

If you are struggling financially, look at your history. You have an abundance block or poverty mindset. Once you get rid of the block, it will be easier to make and manage money.

Never underestimate the power of your life-long dreams. Living your dream can bring you the wealth you desire. You will not know until you open the door to possibilities and opportunities. Begin making your dream a reality.

Save enough money to cover six months' worth of expenses. When emergencies arise, there usually is not time to take out a loan or sell something of value. Keep this money safe and use it only in an emergency.

Make every penny count. Save your change and set it aside in a large container and place. When the container is full, take it to a coin-counting machine, and deposit the money in your account. This makes saving easy and painless.

When it comes to money, pay yourself first with a little bit of savings and then pay for everything else. This helps to ensure that the little sundries do not wind up taking all your income. Put something back for a rainy day first.

Budget is not a four-letter-word. Create a budget and stick to it. Keep track of where and how much you spend to control your money better and save more.

Teach your kids how to save, make, and manage money early in life. When your children learn money basics early, you will not have as many issues with the "I want," and unrealistic expectations when they become teens.

Sell anything you have not used in the last 18 months. Selling these items lets you restructure your priorities. It is a wonderful way to get rid of things you do not use or need while you may have room and money to save or use on other things.

Patiently save for what you want. It is easy to buy out of fear or instant gratification. Put a picture of what you are saving for in a prominent place to help deter you from settling for something you do not really want.

Turn talents, skills, and hobbies into moneymakers. Musicians, hire out your talents for parties. Into woodworking? Sell pre-ordered items. Crochet? Sell your specialty items. Make money from something you enjoy doing.

Know your spending triggers. When you know what emotions and circumstances are most likely to induce you to spend, you can prepare yourself ahead of time and produce a plan of action.

Avoid buying when you are hungry, depressed, tired, or stressed. During these times, you are more apt to spend more money than you intended and make unwise choices.

Do not allow yourself to be persuaded to buy because of a few compliments. Also, walk away when you are being pressured with "limited time" offers. Many sales reps get a commission, and they do not have your best interest at heart.

One person's junk is another person's jewel. Sometimes things are thrown away just because the owner is "tired" of the item. Check out items at "Re" stores or consignment shops to find some great deals and unique items.

Can you rely on it? If you have had the same bank account for a long time, you may be missing new options and rates. Look at your bank's webpage to see what they offer. Contact them to discuss your new options.

Plan meals at least 1-2 weeks in advance. This gives you ample time to shop around and get the best deals.

Organizing Your Life

Clutter steals your peace, limits productivity, and brings a lot of negative baggage with it. Declutter all areas of your life to feel better and work more efficiently, even before you start to organize and optimize.

Declutter first. Everything from emails to garages should be clutter-free. Get rid of the junk before trying to organize. When you see only what you must organize, you can get the job done more quickly.

Keep clutter to a minimum. For each new purchase made, a similar, little-used, or broken item must go. Before you get the latest item, get rid of the old one. This keeps you from being tempted to keep both.

To declutter a room, make it a rule that when you leave the room, you must take something with you and put it in the appropriate place. You are not allowed to leave empty handed.

Place a trashcan in every room. Get creative to make it blend in or conceal the container's real function. This makes it easy to toss things out, just make sure that food, drinks, or wet items always goes to the kitchen trashcan.

Decluttering and organizing makes things easier. Initially this can be time consuming depending on how messy things are. Once you begin to see a little progress, you will feel much better, and you will be initiative-taking to continue.

Tackle one room at a time. Declutter one room and finish organizing it before you start decluttering another room unless someone else is responsible for doing another room. This helps you to stay focused and work effectively.

Once a room has been organized fully, it is easy to do a quick run-through daily to tidy things up. However, if you make sure you put things back and tidy up before you leave the room, it may only take 5-minutes or less per day.

Declutter the kitchen first. This is one of the high traffic areas, so it is also one of the most important rooms to do first. Go through every drawer and cabinet getting rid of items you do not use at least once a year, or it is out of date.

Once the entire kitchen contains only the things you use, start organizing the items. Group and store things by type/usage. For instance, sort and place dishes close to the table or the stove. This optimizes your time and space.

Keeping things organized gives you less time to worry or over-think things. When you spend time organizing your life and all the areas, you also feel better because of your accomplishments.

Make cleanup easy. In every room, have a consistent, preferably hidden, place where you store a dry rag, spray bottle, and/or wet wipes. This helps you to take care of quick cleanups, which is great when someone just pops in.

If you have stacks of unmarred magazines, remove any address label, and donate them to the library, school, or community centre. Unsubscribe from magazines that no longer interest you or serve a purpose.

Use a day planner to keep your day on track as well as your to-do lists. They come in all sizes including palm-size, billfold-size, notebook size, and larger. This makes it easy to always keep a planner with you to stay on track.

Get and use a family planner. When you know what other family members' schedules are, you do not have to put off decisions or activities until you can find out. Being able to make immediate decisions is a huge time-saver.

Consider using a 3-ring binder for the family planner and create a section for each person in it. Keep the planner in a work area or next to a home phone. This allows you to make edits easily and quickly.

Create a schedule and plan for everyone in the family planner. Make a copy of each person's weekly plan and place it on the refrigerator or whiteboard for all to see. This makes it super easy to see the big picture.

Use the COPE method to make people and task organizing simple. COPE is an acronym for Capitalize, Organize, Prioritize, and Energize. Using this method helps to make you a great family manager and keep on top of things.

Capitalize on the ability of every family member to help with age-appropriate household chores. Do more for your kids by doing less for them. Write chores on individual and family chore planners.

Organize and optimize your cooking chores. Incorporate meal planning and bulk cooking into your routine. When you do this, you do not waste time trying to figure out what to have for dinner. It is in the freezer just waiting for you.

Organize your home to make locating and storing things simple. When you store things in a logical place that is close to where you use it, finding an item when you need it becomes an easy decision, even for kids.

Time Management

Instead of making a to-do list, try making a list for today only. This helps you to focus on the top priorities.

Are you a multi-tasking addict? Trying doing one thing at a time. It is amazing how much you can accomplish when your attention is not divided. Staying focused on one thing until it is complete is a remarkably effective strategy.

If you do not get everything on your to-do list finished, start a new list for tomorrow. Put the remaining items in order of importance on this new list. Watch how this one little shift will be effective.

Instead of trying to cram everything into one day, try chunking your time. Time-chunking works better than having no plan at all.

If you procrastinate, ask yourself of what you are afraid. You made me afraid of not being perfect. Once you deal with and fix an underlying issue, you will be less likely to put things off until later.

If you are creative, time management can be a challenge. Practice time management skills daily, to create a new habit.

Create a schedule for your day, week, and month. When you have an extended plan, even if it is tentative, it allows you to make the most of your available time and balance your responsibilities throughout the month.

On your calendar, include all appointments, meetings, and tasks. Assign each item a start time and end time. Limiting the time for each item helps you to stay on schedule.

Reward yourself when you arrive on time or meet a deadline. Rewarding yourself reinforces positive behaviour so you try to do it more often.

Get yourself an accountability partner to hold you accountable for your timeliness. You will quickly be managing time more effectively.

Remember your childhood. You did not have much say-so about what you did or how you did it. You do now. Weigh your options and the consequences of each one, carefully to make the most of your limited time.

Ask yourself if you are putting too much effort into one area and not enough into another. Being conscious of the possibility and tracking what you do will help you discover the answer, especially when you assess out your suspicions.

What can you do to maximize your time? Figure out what takes up too much of your time. Create a plan containing several options that enable you to complete the task in less time.

Take a break. You do not have to sit with something endlessly to get it done. Take 5-minute breaks every hour and reset your energy clock.

Use your commute to your advantage. Meditate, listen to uplifting audio, add lists or memos to your phone, read emails, and more. When you make the most of the time you have, you will have more leisure time to enjoy.

Promise yourself you will not start another project until you finish the ones you already have. Make a priority list and complete each one in that order.

Put a timer on activities, which tend to steal your time. It is okay to take a break, but it is not okay to *get lost* in time.

If you enjoyed this book and learnt from it too,

Why not then go on-line to write a review.

I am just a home-based author with No "big marketing company" behind me, so I highly appreciate your reviews, and it only takes a minute to do.

To submit a sweet review:

- Just go to Amazon and under the BOOKS category, search this book's title or search my name 'Sue Feldman' to get to the product detail page for this book (or click on the book cover photo).

- Click '**write a customer review**' in the Customer Review section.
  - Click '**Submit**'

See all the books I have written at….

www.amazon.com/author/sue.feldman

Please Follow Me.

Thank you in advance!

Sue Feldman

Today start your
day with a smile,
calmness of mind,
coolness of emotions,
and a heart filled
with gratitude.

-Anonymous

365

Affirmations

Confidence
Self-Esteem

Book 2

Sue Feldman